Tiger runs away

Story by Annette Smith
Illustrated by Meredith Thomas

"This is your new home, Tiger,"
said Rebecca to her cat.
"You will like it here."

But Tiger did **not**
like the new house.

3

It did not look
like his old house,
and it did not smell
like his old house.
He jumped away from Rebecca,
and ran out the door.

"Tiger, come back!" said Rebecca.

"Mom!   Tiger has got out.
He has run away!" said Rebecca.
"Mom, come and help me find him!"

"Here we are," said Mom.

Rebecca jumped out of the car and ran to play on the swing.

"Meow."

13

"Meow," said Tiger.

"Mom! Here's **Tiger**! He has walked all the way back **here**!" said Rebecca.

"Oh, Tiger! You are a clever cat," said Mom.

"He looks hungry,"
said Mom.

"Come on, Tiger,"
said Rebecca.
"You are coming back
to the new house
with us."